eight+six

KEN EDWARDS

eight+six

REALITY STREET
2003

Published by
REALITY STREET EDITIONS
4 Howard Court, Peckham Rye, London SE15 3PH
www.realitystreet.co.uk

Some of these poems have appeared, often in modified form, in the following journals: *And, First Offense, Fragmente, Hanging Loose, Nineties Poetry, Neon Highway, Oasis, Object Permanence, PN Review, The Poet's Voice, Rustic Rub, SubVoicive Poetry, Talisman, Terrible Work, Tongue to Boot, Vertical Images, West Coast Line.* "One to One" and "One to Many", translated into Lithuanian by Laurynas Katkus, appeared in the weekly journal *7 Meno Dienos.* "Absconscion" appeared in *Uncommon Ground: the music of Michael Finnissy* (Ashgate, ed. Henrietta Brougham, Christopher Fox and Ian Pace), and "The Purloined Letter" appeared in *Pieces for Howard Skempton* (Spanner, ed. Allen Fisher). The sequence "I Go To Sleep"–"Like" appeared under the title *I Go To Sleep*, first as a Short Run pamphlet (ed. Kelvin Corcoran) and then as Poetical Histories 36 (ed. Peter Riley). The "A Wedding" sequence, minus the final poem, appeared as a pamphlet, *A Wedding* (Red Pagoda Press, ed. Craig Czury). My thanks to all the editors involved.

The cover, designed by the author, shows poem XLVII by Sir Thomas Wyatt, rendered into Zapf Dingbats.

Printed & bound
by Antony Rowe Ltd

A catalogue record for this book is available from the British Library

ISBN: 1-874400-25-3

Mostly for Elaine

And each of us knows that our *self* does not amount to much.

J-F Lyotard,
The Postmodern Condition: A Report on Knowledge

The physicist's atoms will always appear more real than the historical and qualitative face of the world, the physico-chemical processes more real than the organic forms, the psychological atoms of empiricism more real than perceived phenomena, the intellectual atoms represented by the "significations" of the Vienna Circle more real than consciousness, as long as the attempt is made to build up the shape of the world (life, perception, mind) instead of recognising as the source which stares us in the face and as the ultimate court of appeal in our knowledge of these things, our *experience* of them.

M Merleau-Ponty,
Phenomenology of Perception

DARKLY SLOW*

Bring back the persons! I
Ups & says
               they are bipolar & splendid
The jogger in the park, the murderer in the dark
They're so lonely, they speculate, give em something to do
The imaginary persons right here
Wherever that may be, beloved, awed
And in a cloud (a crowd)
                   he she & you
Catching the eye, ordering a round for the unknowables

Bring em all back, I don't want to see them go
One's at a university in the snow
Another on the beach, one praying for the souls in woe
Oh sad poet please be on your toes
The boat casts off, the buddleia grows
And what's behind the moment's horizon no-one knows

* The title is a direct translation of Elliott Carter's "Adagio Tenebroso".

THE ANTHROPIC PRINCIPLE

This is not me (says Me)
a terpsichore of invention, it is what I
says or transforms to blaze or daze
as in the sun or certain main-sequence stars
which make the carbon of "my" culture
whither it becomes the social body
through ratio & constant* that could have been
no other number.
                        And for our next
a jump-technology of reference
that changes, hazes
come down to us through the FM band
Oh the trombones bark
        The forest is young again
                So fill me [_____] in

* Planck's Constant (6.6262×10^{-34}) governs the nucleosynthetic process
by which stars convert hydrogen to the heavier elements of which we are
made.

LAMBENTLY FLUID

Is there a better way of saying this?
I hope so. Did the dog
beg her master for the stick
to be thrown? And did she give
unconditional love, obeisance, abasement?
Did summer come & go?
Were resources wasted? Did the park
turn from green to brown & back to green?
Do any here know what they are, can we ever know, these
    intangibles of comfort
their cheeks to our jowls, who sometimes stay with us for a
    while but eventually
get up & go, allowing others to join us in their turn, & still
    others after them
the spaces cumulating until finally they too take their leave
    & all is as before?

LUNAR HOLOGRAPHY

Did you see our shadow creep up on the moon* stealing a
bite of luminosity? That was Thursday — well
I write this in the interim or do I mean
the ante-room where it seems as though I'm slowly being
rotated under a bright light did you
ever get that feeling? When you are no longer there
each trip, a rare adventure in prospect
ends the same way, mildly toxic, no problem

Ghosts in the plumbing, fox rot in the suburban verge
beer & biriani would do it — or not, for I am
wrecked without you and would have you return forthwith.
I send packages into that ether men do call foreign
parts, hoping for reciprocity — what comes back:
the "Don't panic" code, smoke moving behind the lights

* Lunar eclipse visible in London, 9/10 December 1992.

THE ENGINE OF LOVE

Dark drizzle falls & falls the sparkling dark
rain falls as evening falls on the football pitch
on the Ex-Servicemen's Club & Social Centre
where bitter's a pound a pint & where talk too
is cheap on a Saturday night — as over the table
over the numbered balls a boy confronts
his Dad who grips the cue in his big fists —
the boy's eyes flash with anger
                                        at this moment
for the first time he drives the engine of love
but he's out of control — he pleads for its return —
beer spills on mica, video talk resumes
outside rain logs into the abandoned turf
great pylons march without a motion to
the power station on the distant coast

THE PANIC MUSEUM
(*Theory of Poetry*)

Falling to pieces in this brilliant backwater
with 800 years of delusions washing around me
now I lose track of the evening session
as conversations disconnect behind me.

I'd spent too much time placing out the plastic chairs
I decided, for the audience that would never come:
folk from the ante-room, burning with rhetoric
the liquidated stock in the panic museum.

First among them being the pope of fright
absent as always, though here in his manor he
's passed the law to his clones to keep safe.

(Watched by drunk students, two swans drift in moonlight
asleep on the placid water their necks plunged through
their feathers (they did not change my life).)

TO THE ESTUARY

To the estuary's wooden hulks I travel
along the sandlings where animals cry again
bass lines of bombers again over
dance fields over the class system of old England.
It is essential the trappings are slowly stripped away
hydrochloric acid is useful for this or a blowtorch or
some dead good corrosive so that through the foggy air
I may again believe this was not what I saw:

A quantity of animal dung in the bottom of the boat
a lighted doorway again I am in
the summer house in autumn where shapes move
in unison or conflict we look in and on and over
through and from where the paint burns
a sheen into the soft-hard air in England's daylight

ABOVE THE SHINING ROOFS

I had the air about me   Fractured
Greyish in the sodium lamplight
in front of the Rye Hotel   Oh gentle pint!
Oh friend oh lifestyle choice!

Outward in a zigzag
from the Cambrian beach this once was
ambience plunged towards the zero degree
of the bathroom shelf

From a higher energy state in negative space
the lights had come on one by one
to make of monochrome those great

rich blacks   Above the shining roofs I swear
as god is my fax machine
hung tears or drops of golden blood

TREMBLING IN THE BERSERK STATION

Today came to life at 6.30 am, found him
trembling in the berserk station
where he remained until 6.50, then got up
in darkness to hunt for a shirt.

Out at 7.08 in remnants of freezing fog
first the newsagent's then onward still —
The fog hung heavily in hollows round tracks
as the train pulled out towards the light

Suppose you were trying to do something
impossible, like, from memory that isn't there —
Suppose ... well then it wouldn't be healing so much

as being already well
or stepping out of the time track
in which the disease occurs.

BECOMING

You see that to come into your own
is not an easily achievable wish
falling within its own allusive rubric
for you yourself are still the helpless baby
or a housecat scratching at upholstery
in the quite awful confines
of your history & ceremony
the source of all that stuff you hate so much.
But, luminous with wine, you watch
the one lying on the hospital bed & your image
mirrored, and slowly it becomes less hard:
the window is a source of light too, after all,
the architecture & the plan
become more clear: it's not you not you...

I GO TO SLEEP

I go to sleep in the railway buildings
which someone said looks like a boat
For five years I had that fine panorama
spread out before me until winter came with
sunny chill I wore my leather put it in a poem
I went to sleep & woke to oh just mountains
of phone messages & somehow after that
things were not quite the same
                                    Look — I want
to put this & this & those
together so it has a thing inside the line
(the dark line that flits & jags)
which maybe is what I call poetry who can
say, which is no fugue & which is mine

THE CORAL NECKLACE*

Then we take the path on down the valley
accompanied perhaps by a hopeful dog
through all that tumbling fecundity of oak & alder
fir & pine, & eucalyptus, vetch, wild lilies
lemons ripening in their picture cage of netting
& in the bend before us the sea glistening hazy still the
Siren rocks amid it pink & purple white
so there we drink our water

Now I've opened the curtains this a.m.
& it's frozen upon the garden
a shade encroaching hard on fugitive glitter
How a year can go by, then another
it's in the earth somewhere, ochre & silver
sometimes your tongue can taste the coast

* Sorrento and London, May 1993, and six months later...

I GO TO SLEEP (2)

I go to sleep in the railway buildings
                              whereupon
a child appears, shining amid design specifications
says press space bar now
                         I am a directory called stenosis
recalling mental sex as though the pointing device
had gone berserk all values had come out
as surplus value   But I remember being that child
discovering the sentence in the midst of speaking it
which was a very intelligent and a human thing

I go to sleep in England but where do I wake up?
for blood travels to my face and darkens my perception
into a sulcus of unwavering belief which is stupid stupid
I go to sleep as the fabric shivers
the aircraft shimmers the sentence dissolves
into the ultra-violet

MANAGEMENT DEVELOPMENT

He comes & goes into & out of your
spectrum of issue avoidance, & that's cool
it's what you want & don't want in the opera
of your craving for the new
and no less than totally interesting, saying yes
you'd love to & meaning it, speaking of wanting to go
there with him as well but not wanting
to get too close, not great, but all we have

You clearly saw & it's OK it really is

You did like them & put them on

I had to say this sooner or later & in the end
as good as did though you'll agree "as good as"
isn't as good as
          so you could bat the charge right back to me
but didn't   & I love that in you too

LIKE

My love is like

Oh no it isn't

And its loss is like

For heaven's sake

Like, what if it were all a
big mistake?

Because you're jealous & so
judgemental

You can't talk to me like that
what can I say

Because you have some
personal opera going on

Its music, what, huge
like a locomotive
imaged at strange resolutions

No   Nothing like that

It's too luminous a conceit?

It's enough to change the
shape of a man's head

It hurts like fuck
it hurts my, like, human heart
you know what I mean

I mean nothing is like anything else*

* This line is stolen from Eric Mottram. Something always to bear in mind.

23

AMERICAN MUSIC

When Jimmy Cobb hit that high cymbal*
when the metal went liquid & blue
all the cats in the farmyard woke from golden slumbers
in the twilight of money†
                            Now
there ain't nobody here but us (white) chickens
beside the red wheelbarrow
Oh that doesn't work any more, this farm's not so funny
ripped & jammed up on which so much de-

pends like in the west it's always after the
war the junk belief jammed up the thing
his thing my thing our thing the changes
kind of hard edged pursuivant on strange information
Oh Jimmy Cobb oh Frank O'Hara we're waiting
for you, get up get it on
do the business —

* Jimmy Cobb, drummer with the Miles Davis band, 1958-63. The
cymbal shot referred to comes 1'30" into "So What" on *Kind of Blue*,
right on Miles' entry; as everybody knows, this was the moment when the
world went from monochrome into colour.
† "In the twilight of money" is a phrase attributed to Le Corbusier.

SHIPWRECKED AND COMATOSE

Euphoria I hear you calling
Euphoria begins to wash off
leaving a pale petulance at such roughage
that seeps between — no more —
this is a tradition I just invented
all for you. Excuse me have we finished
discussing this yet? You, a woman of my
own age? Or something?
So that now I feel the ennui of one who hasn't had much
congress with real persons
Who is dull with sun & bluster on a charabanc trip to the
seaside on Bank Holiday Monday
The faint hope lurking that distorts judgement Euphoria
come back it's OK I'll make a deal with you

CHAMBER MUSIC*

You have a great wide window Chris through which
sunbeams flash, reverberate on four
white walls a dark stained floor — it's a good
window for a good & useful space
Now we're tuned up — but I just want to say
The Art of Fugue's not something to be hacked through
as one might chainsaw a viola in half
by some careless mischance (finding oneself
with the wrong implement for the occasion)
                                        Hey

what is this piece of wood doing in my hands?
where am I? You mean the city's turned &
summer's coming through?
                        Welcome to

Planet Earth —
home of Johann Sebastian Bach

* For Chris Shurety, on his 50th birthday.

DELICIOUSLY FAUVE

Summer heat
envelops the flimsies
the thing you did, the number five
shooting straight, deliciously fauve
you wanted one of those, I wanted
to remake them all with my corrections
oh it's so sweet to be listing on the wing
just give the man a smoke he needs a boost that thing
wasn't right, I need coating with foil after
such a marathon, with brightness to
reflect the summer's heat and
keep from dehydration
under big glass & no
sense of time

THEY DIDN'T GO HOME

The poets and their entourages, appendages,
readerships, theoretical props and absences
are variously and severally assembled.
A shows pictures and reads the words.
B takes seriously the notations in cowboy comic balloons.
C vacillates, and comes down on the side of externality.
D demonstrates conviviality (again).
E emphasises the smallness of the audience.
F is quiet and has with him a pair of roller blades.
G, as usual, enigmatic.
H waxes shaven.
I have had my hair newly cut but have forgotten about it.
Sound travels from the street below because it is a warm
night & there is no reason for folks to go home.

THE POETS GATHER
(*Theory of Poetry 2*)

The poets gather. They, like poetry itself,
want to be, not seem. Which is seemly.
These are their stories, and the summation
of them is this: that they reject story.
Why, they are paralytic with joy: on their plastic chairs
they identify the depth of field of such paradoxes
and exult in it — they presuppose no need
for emotional closure.
That was then. And now?
Well, only you & I are left, and we're engaged
in refutation. Yours is a pint of bitter,
mine's a Guinness. This proposition is true. We raise
our glasses, we refute it
and refute again.

SHIFTS GENRE OFTEN*

The poet is one who commits
acts of barbarism out of
social urgency. She babbles
and is a rejection of the
language of. She keeps the context
problematic, pivots as often
as possible, which permits
the tide. This is kind of lingo
phrase for those sorts of people lost
in "the water of the river"
when the water *is* the river.
Its maps are metamorphic not
atemporal, a comedy of
metonymic chains, of logics

* For Lyn Hejinian, some of whose presentation in the King's Talks series, King's College London, April 1998, I have paraphrased freely here.

BECOME GEMS HERE

The map has got scrambled & we are all
delighted. My foot is ambiguous, it has
locationality but not
positionality. Don't stop. "Those useful choreographies
can easily become a baleful aerobic"* and
once the stultifiers have a hex on warp agencies
who knows where it'll end up?
But I am certain of a noble uncertainty, it's OK

now I see that you in your way
radiate and this is legal & good.
And everyone says you got the look
of the artist formerly known as god.
We are conversant with our glorious plangent mess
gazing rapidly past this which into here

* The quotation is attributed to Cris Cheek in New Hampshire,
September 1996

SMITHEREENS

This pen has a good sheen to it, or as they say
it's cute as a sack of cash — so in the Rye
Hotel surrounded by smithereens* of popular culture
he set down to write the story of his life.
At my elbow is the most sinister suit I've
seen in a very long while he says these threads is
regal, tell him I'm tied up Mandy I am
shirted & cufflinked up don't get all previous
with me!
         The bar hots up it's actually been
shanghai'd by sweating napes not even a legal
eagle'd wreak a blue streak what can I say?
I meet the brain-dead & the children of the
brain-dead I am among them all the week

* Parts of speech jostling for last orders in Peckham. The shade of the
boxer Chris Eubank is lurking in a corner.

PUISSANT CAR

Like a dickhead in a BMW
he presumes too much — and this presumption
is his puissant car — with copious clocks
and microprocessors, extreme of function.
A male cadence says "just do it" and unkeen
to seem too couth he stupefiedly
obeys and makes the death hex sign to gain
consumer satisfaction, sucked & seen.

My friend! that self-same powerhead within
the chrome & polished steel his glorious armour
was I — gearstick in hand — no, but you can
imagine — liquid years and laddish glamour
faded, carless in Peckham, on your pins
hearing the engine of grace slowly turn over

SPEAKS INTO MOBILE

Striped of shirt & lambent of tie speaks
into mobile a pipette of value wants to
plug a surf belladonna, becoming
cyclonic, cumuli pile onto his prospect
the heterosexual object of his
desire now once again forbidden
or unrepresentable, smash her face
and centre spread in colour.
COME ON YOU LOVEBIRDS get real
get fucked become the business
take me to your leader, plastic
Schubert in a basket with all the trimmings,
soften my head into the soup of the day
wank to the fascinoma of the month

CLICK ON THIS

Show me your gold card & I'll show you
my hymen. The modelling of desired behaviours
by a respected role model, irradiated or
genetically modified, can be a key determinant

in changing the whole tone scale
of an individual's attitudes & fragrance.
It is important that this lost language, these
lost sounds are flooded with options.

It is important that these ambient behaviours
are linked to values & competencies, mobile
and integrated into our noise-aspect,

appraisal and fractured management
corporate policies. I have read & understood
and agree to the terms & conditions.

I GO TO SCHOOL IN YOUR BONES*

Sex me up, my shape (she-ape!) of risk
tune up your heels to a serious reciprocity
give me all the attention of your imaginary fingers
like parachute silk in the troposphere.
I refer to your lustrous presence on my arms
where the veins go — apparently distant events —
high scent does enter the frame, with great velocity
I believe it to be nonsense, or else certainty.

Turn up the sound map, a social body
dirtied over from the inheritance
of chaos and loving invention.
Bring me treble clef & metaphor
bind my thresholds and to hell with balance.
Never let I speak —

* Title taken from Clarissa Pinkola Estés, *Women Who Run with the Wolves*

WINDOWS FOR DOGS

Thou art my ape, my cynosure,
my star, my dog's bollocks. Mica
winks in the paving stones, my
fingers remember the number

and send graphics, text files & other
information to John. Fibrillating
and seriously flaky. Saw heron fly
onto and perch on a rooftop:

Tulse Hill. More than seven
melodies simultaneously
become chaotic. Two thousand

years pass. An incoming fax. John,
John. The hoarding trembles in the
wind and startles the dog.

PECKHAM PULSE

In the dusk filled street a man
is up to his wrists in engine.
The Church of Strong Prayer trades
straplines with the Beneficial Veracious
Christ Church. A bad child loudly
bruises the glass. Such journeys
are unbearable from the day they
are born. Something wrong.

Establishing shot across West Africa.

Braids filled with circuits
swing past the shops in holy
brand awareness, bound
to the logic board. Previously unknown
species re-invade.

BROADLY THROUGH THE EYES OF HIS CONTEMPORARIES

When the film's projected backwards
    mother rises feet-first
from the pool, the twins recede &
    in time all is lost.

White leader, sprocket flicker
    transferred to VHS. Friendship
decays into an exchange of influence
    and services. Chaos follows, then poetry.

Sluice down those monkeys! Put
    the doll back into dark winter,
ramp down the glory. Have key words
    drift from one frame to the next,
but have them marked up as
    unstable & prime for flunking.

HIGGLEDY PIGGLEDY

Back from the deed to the word, no that is
back from the dead to the world
to the brouhaha of bumpy dancers
messed-up tactical dogs & their sunk pints
he crash into the most awful trope in the continuum
on a thin story, not your fault —
Do me a privilege, avoid the brokers
click on here & you're away.
And so how's business? are you sure?
privy to what? the radius of delirium?
Would you say slumped or dumped or
occupationally hazarded? The dancers part company
with their clothes, flatter to deceive, turnover
sluggish — can I do escape?

WITHOUT BELIEF

To keep going on like this how can you live
like this without borders in your head*
as if you were a mollusc or an angel?
The secret's not to try too hard for it's
impossible no chance when everything's
so pitiably sensible & glitters
or fragments in contrast with its label
before attaining maximum velocity

Well I'm not a technical sort of person
in that sense although I'd like to think so —
all I know's sometimes you have this feeling
of architecture, that is, big things heavy
things — and other times there's nothing but
the loudness in your ears or skull of blood

* Some phrases taken from a magazine interview with the improvising
guitarist Caspar Brötzmann.

THE DEEP ECOLOGY OF SPECIAL FX

In the dead weather
before the storm
in fields where copper
flows like butter

as though a small winged
insect were in there
wanting egress
your chest flutters.

In dead television time
a ghost highway links
somewhere to nowhere.

You don't want to be there
but it isn't there — it's here
and there's no place else to go.

ITS EVER MOVING SHADOWS

Because I believe in violence lies the answer
and often we have called this love
when I am standing in the light
among the indeterminate connectives
and you come towards me to this blaze that rages
then I touch you on the side of the torso
and on the arm & your face that gazes —
Should I reach your eyes
                                    — but who can say —
I go to sleep in the railway buildings,
patterns of blood flow in the brain
float like surfaces over every ground,
I close my eyes in the transparent universe*
that casts its ever moving shadows —
You have to be lost before you can be found

* According to Steven Weinberg in *The First Three Minutes*, the universe
became transparent to radiation at about 700,000 years of age.

BIG ROOM

You head for the big room always
tending to lose your marbles at any minute
I can't believe how you —
but shucks, you do have a good eye*
and in & under your wide contemplative sky
if going this way & that you miss
what's closest at hand, ie the thing itself, well then, you can
outstare its palpability
        By contrast, being a man from the south I'm
        almost all colour & sound from the inside
        signifying what? who cares (I do)
        I come to the power plant & am entranced
        with the difficulty of it & your actual enigma
        You bury your head in its clouds

* The enigma of looking.

CHAOS THEORY

South East England contains about 17 people
(and two of these are you & me)
sustainable development, inflated property values.
But we now live in a disinflationary world.

Parts of Arabia had a wet end to last week,
King Khalid military city measured 47mm.
This means downsizing and de-layering
for us, my dear, I'll wager.

You can choose between the headless chickens,
metal with a golden sheen.
It's not that bad, we're talking small percentages.
Over North America, unusual temperatures
made the headlines —
I've a residential cadence yet —

RUG

The business between us is what matters
the recurrent iron & stone the I & the you
and the who and why & whither, a fibre of sense
that oscillates between us we hold onto.
Let's weave that into a metaphor shall we
about six by four, say, a material base
to do the business, the season a little dusty
the night grown old — you want to imagine the rest

Well how's it going and are you ready now

And do you remember how utterly

And was there a time when it might have been

No — there isn't an end to this dialogue, nor will
there be, the stone & iron the iron & stone
again I stand foursquare on the rug you pull

HOLDING MY HEART STILL

If I were endlessly
scrutable you could
follow me there
or here — the geography
is immaterial. Then
you could tell me
very gently
what it was

I wanted
        /
            didn't want
to know:
the story
behind the
story.

I GO TO SLEEP (3)

Dreaming on tan plush
I view the colour spectrum
the unnecessary repetition
of limiting gestures.
Even now, sentient
screensavers flicker
blindly, false cognates
on the field.

Rooted to the spot
with a mouth full
of language, I am scuppered
by the logic bombs
of double curvature.
O tempora, o fucking mores.

MELANCHOLY

Darling person, whom I had not seen
for many months, I have forgotten so & so's
name, and my words slow down & echo
under the bridge which makes you laugh
it seems as though I am to come to a dead stop.
When things loomed large, we all went mental
with passing & movement, the pageantry
and all that business, when things were future
I mean *in* the future, or of it —
Then quite suddenly it's over, I am a child hearing
Beethoven in the street the evening of Xmas Day
or from summer's vantage watching fall approach, only the years
overlay, and suddenly too there are not many more
to come, my darling person: meetings, partings:

THE BOOK DIGS INTO MY SKIN

The book digs into my skin & flesh
talks in tongues of petal sound, squeak vapour & dog barks logic
everywhere setting still goes on
when I wasn't quite making sense.
Been down the road & had the man show me
eight machines, feel the strain in my upper body now.
I tried to contact you, but the pulses disappeared
into virtual space, bruising the rationals
all over again, like loops, like dogs, a wind spirals the dust up
"We had magic and
smoke and lots of theater action at that time".*
And then the clocks went back, the lights
went solid rearranged my dental arc into a locked proscenium.
Soon it will be winter you don't reply

* Taken from *Mixtery,* a festschrift for Anthony Braxton, edited by
Graham Lock (Stride, 1995).

SLAKED BY PUBLIC WATER

You are old, father tortoise
spending your end of summer days on a spar
or impersonating one in the
municipal sun of the municipal pond of the
municipal park.*
And there no dog can catch you, prise open your shell
which is a blessing as well as a disguise
when you're practically insensible
and waiting for it to be over.

So that's pretty well it for the season,
planes, sycamores, elders tremble on the brink of shedding
and the goslings almost grown go by on the gloss.
The end of this story is at hand
& is not known

* Peckham Rye Park, perhaps close by where the young Blake saw a host
of angels in a tree.

THEY DESCRY WORDS, THEIR SHADOWS

Goodbye my friends it flows dusks sadly
and reality drops like a stone.
Some members of the group said they admired
someone or something dear to them, it matters
not who was inspired, fit onto standard
postcard size. The liminal space recedes
the question poses limpid as a cry
too late, sat in a garden, one of forks.
                                So change the script:
The lid falls off the zapper slowly dark
this is where you begin to take apart —
Courage! make stint in the alarm
those impossible journeys struck to brighter lands
at times peaceful and at times without effort

INTERROGATION ROOM REMIX*

The pillar perished is whereto I leant

A human electricity a great
Generous boom a list

From east to west still seeking though he went

In this grey/yellow space
I sense you
In your best bruiser skin — believe me there's
An alibi in one —

Of all my joy the very bark and rind

In the grey space what I remember's this

The strongest stay of mine unquiet mind
My mind in woe, my body full of smart

And books to read before it grew too late

What can I more but have a woeful heart

* In memoriam Eric Mottram, 1924-95. With some help from Sir
Thomas Wyatt, poem CLX sampled from *Collected Poems*, OUP 1975.

AFTER BERLIOZ

Silence ... rustle of young wheat
cry of quail
a bunting pouring forth
profound peace ... a dead leaf.

Life seemed so very far away
a thing apart
flashed & glinted in the mountings
over there.

And the fit
tearing up handfuls of grass
the crushing sense
of absence
takes possession
as if a vacuum had formed.

EXECUTIVE SUMMARY

This box of bone & matter
    is
        in the reception area
messaging   speaks into mobile

Friendship decays
                feels inadequate to
even so
        even this vestige, recombinant

Check:
        press hash 9
then the extension number desired

        fractured,
      her body exploded
as the ground hit it

THE PURLOINED LETTER*

Beginning the mountain
with the first basket of earth
is good science.
Exciting counterpoint
from no less than — to some — to many —
is a statement and no statement at all.
Making less most is enriching extent
and there's the special beginning of it.

For your letter and for your view of that Chinese mountain
my own many thanks.
That we are all in
music we are all in poetry we are all
neophytes is encouraging —
and that in its own way completion is begun.

* For Howard Skempton, on his 50th birthday, rearranging or recycling
his words in a letter to the author, July 1997.

ABSCONSCION*

Stay
As though astonished
Through the rubric of
"The transformation of love"†

In the room
In the rain
How you have been
Many times this way O boy

I don't know if I can
Indure
On the door it says

Use other door
You go through it (the
Turn) and

* For Michael Finnissy, on his 50th birthday, July 1996.
† The phrase is from Rilke's letters.

ASTONISHED IN THE FLOOD*

Stay   as though   to sleep
        What sudden   rubric   ripen
I am a shining   fugitive
        Stay   face and   darken

As though   the known thing   bursts
        Shed energy   rose   froze
Stay tracked   material   personal
        Rare child   depends or   grows

And all our   values hopeful   touch
        That in you   deep   & wanting
To put this   devastated &   to reach

The dark   ally like   slanting
        To each   of us   how much
To sleep   & wake   maybe

* This title from Michael Haslam's *Continual Song*.

AMONG THE LIME KILNS AND DILAPIDATED PLEASURE GARDENS OF LAMBETH*

Bebop   Buddleia   backup   crashing   why
     Bring   brouhaha   haha   to the dark a
Burning   technically   like a   time   the lights
     Don't   sleep   sense   shapesh   fish'n

Sense   sensing   lull to   strengths   precise
     Bi   biped   peddle   in the gel if to
You   You don't   And she   I write   unless
     Always   crashing   matter   casts   undo

Darkly   wrecked   visible   in parts   perflow
     Delirious   radium   of a   had   & hads
Marine   must be   the colours   hereto   grows

Delph   germane   unless   a pretty   crowd
     Crashesh   horrid   pellucid   no one no
Coming   undone   crashing   spun to   cloud

* And this from the pages of Peter Ackroyd's biography *Blake*

59

HIS LAST GASP

You   don't want   but it isn't   there
    As a matter of   muscles   move involuntarily
And   there's nowhere filled in the   somewhere
    Bright   he can be   flash   momentarily

But lets him   know   why   brightness moves
    How he can be   but isn't   fetch the air
Which isn't here   how   devastate behoves
    Of all significant places   personally   rare

Oh known thing   Oh air   that multiplies the known
    Oh technical adventure   given hinterland bestir
Go into vehicle   given   grown

To thrive &   spasm   else to be   gone
    Want is   distance dust hereto   there
Simply suck   illuminate   eliminate   alone

HIS LAST GASP (2)

                              but   isn't
          matter
                      nowhere
      Bright

                  know
                                          the air
Which   isn't
                              person

      know   Oh air
                  adventure   given

To
      Want is   to
                  illuminate

A FRIEND IN NEED

The windows smashed
and the vase
                    that you, a woman thus
Poor Tom —

I love my love with a el
"or maybe shut your face"*
It just isn't fair
                    or graceful

that you should —
oh   my dear
friend in the   world

Oh maybe kiss
before I go to ground in the vertical
desert   like this

* JHP, of course.

FOUR*

One is to become
The other — it never happened
A third — relatively minor
And after all, the last
It did not change my life
From east to west still seeking though he went
Suppose that it, or they, can, will & did or do
Then all would be — otherwise
        If not now when
        If not when, then
        Why
        If not, well then
        How
        But why not now?

* After listening to *The Crowd*, Rova saxophone quartet, Hat Hut CD.
For a far more comprehensive response to the same, see Clark Coolidge's
The Rova Improvisations (Sun & Moon, 1994).

EVENTUALLY GET UP AND GO

Thinking
  lay across one of the thwarts
        how long
           the
        water

And that   it was
they should come
by such a little to   my body

I live   free
and can escape thither when this
        the empty downland then
under the wind
    is a mood that comes to
      myself from the confusion*

* From the final pages of H G Wells` *The Island of Dr Moreau*

SERIOUS JUNGLE

Already bicameral, unflummoxed amid breccia
or is it bric-à-brac, you return to your passions
a quizzical bunny, bouncing to the strange
attractors of the city, parrotty and fruity to boot
        Chromatic with butterflies re-engined for timing
        fashioned to be daffy of absolute value, akimbo
        with the loveliness of an open door
        lashings of snippets dance to your jungle beat
And when you run to the end of the jungle
let not your value be exchanged
let your kilter remain in the limbo of joy
till dusk has reclaimed the farthest shore
Abre las puertas por favor
*quiero olvidar lo que es dolor**

* The last two lines are from a popular song from Ecuador.

BLACK DOG

He steps through the door. The emblems
are on his forehead, the molecules of sadness
in his mouth. I heard laughing & thunder
in the night before he arrived.

How sharply I feel the bite, how quickly
how trembling I make my way over to you
across the long prairie bed, in the
long rumbling dawn that never ends....

In the republic of dreams in the dry bed
in terror as the colours change always
where trash is thrown you menstruate

out of the night the breakers the laughter
the beach at the end of the road that never ends.
I'll wait for you there don't let me down.

THREE

Three is two & one
The octave — never harboured
Or heard — reflectively finer
And before all, the past
"You must change your life"
The pillar perished is whereto I leant
Suppose I had not, turned I did into undo
Then all would be — restored

       If not the one
       Or two, when
       You
       Were not, well then
       Who
       Am I now?

TOO CHICKEN TO TALK TURKEY

I love speech, and most of all
the shape it makes in your mouth.
Or: I love speech, and in particular
the way that your mouth shapes it.

It's your mouth, and mine
and the shapes that emerge
then make a text, or a reply. I wish I could say.
And I am so sorry.
And I rejoice. On the slow curtain, dusk
begins to gather, in the park men walk
their dogs
and the scent of hot wax fades in the room.
Such happiness awaits us.
(This happiness will end.)

RED SHOES

Red shoes black shoes every kind
of shoes *Dance on my friend!* as we elapse
from coma to wakefulness along the river
side we are really just talking and walking and
talking nothing more and nothing more
is needed bursting heart to heart to
think of it! that you should be a friend in the
world is everything (blue shoes a lapsed kiss) —
Who can say
it drifts and skips is fortunate and is
three words your peaceful embouchure
for many years the vertical desert
of the treble clef I think it has been happening
for many years

YOUR PEACEFUL EMBOUCHURE

In respect of a place I loved and was in that
I now return to or open to, it's wonderful
how you in your body
and I in you, how normal it is.
And this becomes a morning you inhabit
always these days as the sun ascends —
it was as though it always has, and is
the love of evermore being guided.
Since it has come to beam on us I find it
in me to cope, packed into small pitches as I am
staggering into & out of my clothes
burning to tell as never before
living to be in the solid deep
swaddled and watching, so early days.

IN THE LIGHT OF

I am   in England but
not of it   you could be
    a travelling player
echo-accoutred   your eyes
glistening with gaze aforethought
in the dark   my head listening
to its own beat or become then aware
of yours the metal device against your good heart.

And there were also
    lambent key sequences, or sequins
against the squeaking floorboard.
Who can recall the light
    of dwelling   in memory before
the thing had happened, even?

BLUE DAY

Brave and excellent as you are, you'll know
what's broached must also be consumed profusely.
All that robust energy, and the narrative on an
arbitrary grid.
                A greybeard named Zeno
                   asks what happened? I don't
recall, he said, I will do some creative work today
but it was too complete and had too much meaning
                  to be useful.
                         Us lugging our rucks
them selling late repros at high prices,
stock collapsed, Niagara in our bellies.
        Soon healed.
Draw the curtains on a blue day today, wield
blue dangerously before it stretches

I'M DOING MY BOOKS ON YOU

Oh pedal point, oh search engine
show me your autumnal grief caboodle
your body at the velocity of zero
your loved voice superimposed.
Oh mobile antenna, heavenly brico-
lage my things, my autumnal things.
No. They are not
mine, they never were, & suddenly there you are:
what mambos what ecliptics
so out of & in control. (The body of course
is one's writing, or properly,
what writes this: it comes from somewhere.)
        Oh pedal point
        Oh embouchure

OUT IN THE VIOLETS

Allure is being cancelled each day as I speak
and I can't hardly talk
       How do us talk
about I & you?

      This box doesn't deserve to think!

They are partly rehydrated
figs ready to eat now

          Out at sea
a rockpool the Dardanelles as a child
peers out on beauty

bells chime & float towards too much

out in the violets & the mud
listening to cuckoos

THE BIRTH SHIP

The lovers are entwined one on the other
breathing together they produce
                              the same note.
Someone cries

        out in the night.   There is nothing
outside themselves
                        This does not
appal them as it should.

They produce offspring
        who grow up eventually and pursue
independent careers.

Someone dies   The window can't
        easily be opened.   Outside
themselves the world moves

MERCY

Throw yourself on my mercy, and I'll throw myself
    upon yours. Then we'll enter into
the summer of it with all due sumptuousness
    and imperturbability. But you
already know this. Here begins the realm
    of the first person plural: *impossibility*
coming into its pomp, the one & the other making
    a collective pronoun of the "enemy self"* —

we cannot know just what *that* person's thinking.
    Here begins the realm of imposs-
ibility, you know it, not that, not that
    but this, that we're immersed in, where
we learn it from, the actual stuff
    not rockets & bells, not that, but this,
                              this...

* Laura Riding, "As Many Questions As Answers".

A DREAM OF RECLAIMED LAND

Time knows it   equivalence knows it
the filth know it   mine host behind the bar
knows it   the helix of language knows it
surplus value knows it   the boys who
take care of these things know it
Mary Quite Contrary, the twin strikers, the midnighters
all know it   Trace who is 4 Gary knows it
numbers melody mayhem & transformation know it

But you my beauty who find yourself in a place
vastly crammed with incident and resource, and see
no way out of it, you do not know it.
You venture onto "reclaimed land" but it's dark to you:

ahead, huge buildings with screens on which luminous text
scrolls & forever transforms, yet seems hardly to change.

YOU MOVE YOUR HANDS

Oh my
       dearest person what it is you mean
to me and all
       that I entail —

To awaken in the early
       hours of the day near the
loved one
       it is too much to bear.

Crotales. Untuned percussion. From afar:
       ostinati, the return of thunder.
Then a low, held note.

You move your hands
       in the air   like this —
You shine from the face outward.

A WEDDING*

       flowered out of nowhere
and overwhelmed
       the groundwork –
it's just that events conspired.
A thin sliver of pale blue on the western
horizon & a white cotton shirt
over the heart.
       And so it proved

The path of totality
       brought us here†
to the churchyard. The bloom
       of voices came
through. Once & for all
       it was

* The following sequence uses material from Stravinsky's "Les Noces".
† Solar eclipse partly visible in London, 11 August 1999.

A WEDDING (2)

On Wednesday the corona
On Thursday a strange & hilarious day
On Friday my green gardens are blooming
On Saturday the sky was fresh

O braid my
          light-brown braid
I plaited you mechanically
          with the words of consolation.
One braid
becomes two,
          the army
of mechanicals
          arrive –
          attacca subita

A WEDDING (3)

And so it proved: they approached
in such a space, believing that
this time was never to have arrived.
But, having come, it stays just long enough

to make a resonance in the air.
          Speech forms,
a trumpet line ascends into
imaginary sunlight at the clerestory.

The tablecloth
The corona the
return of war –

Abstraction: the imaginary
          combination
of line & light

A WEDDING (4)

Someone is choosing his words
      Sudden rain, and thunder
We're loose in a room
      Someone plucks up courage
to be composed, to be where
nobody expected. Another fumbles
and a third says
      "Take your time"

A hand, a flower, a sweet,
a fruit, a violet, short-lived,
unannounced.

Someone moves across
the garden, as she'd done when a girl.
That was in the photograph.

A WEDDING (5)

We are talking as
night returns, "I
don't know whether
I can get to
sleep." We shall have to
get into our clothes,
go out, post letters,
return as though

Sparrow to sparrow
lay a sound
upon a sound.
We live by day
& night, we practise
hospitality.

A WEDDING (6)

but here there is only a
light breeze ruffles the
       water out of
       darkness —

The future returns
with enhanced
       energy
as a consequence of it,
       money
dwindling, weather changeable.
Someone takes a picture,
someone
       is full of business, gradually
the clouds dispersed

TWO

Now am I whom artifice
Supposes? Were you then, two
Or one if not restored? well then
Would all undo into I did,
Pitch into bliss, had I not turned?
The pillar perished is whereto I leant
Your change must be before all, relatively heard
Or harboured, octave one & two

       If not this, then
       This
       A pair, as one —
       Or not, the one
       And two
       Is one

ONE TO ONE: NOURISHMENT

On a blue day, one has food and passes it to
the other. It's a spoon, and there is food on it.
Dirt is postponed. Each is halfway between.
The food is made of molecules — proteins & fats —
it enters and is appropriate to the function, it
does not overstay. The gesture is one of
appeasement, of intimacy and proferred friendship.
Tombstones come down, milk forms, it's only

human. One begins and the other completes
the task begun. Receiving is likewise,
reciprocal sluices: the other responds generously
to the one, and this is what was intended. You are
valued, for your lips curl round my gift.
What is freely offered

ONE TO MANY: INTERPRETATION

We are constituted, and so we are free.
Who says? The person whose voice
so distorts that no information is conveyed?
And the others, assembled on this platform
or that one, contemplating icons, of a morning?
It's windy. Delays are occurring. Globalisation
occurs. In Antarctica, an iceberg the size of
Wales starts to break up.

The broadcast server will close down
in 1 minute — please save your data.
This is security. The fire alarm tests
have now been completed and
normal procedures are back in operation.
You have new mail waiting.

MANY TO ONE: SOUND PRODUCTION

Extremely rapid & akin. Dental tremoli:
the lower jaw trembles to create amplitude.
There is extensive use of glissandi. I love
the way in which the air is set in motion
in the movements of the organs in which
it vibrates between. It is as if coupled,
turns on the role, the middle & final
metamorphic hinges where the text shape changes.
Her virtuosity deployed, each sound is followed
by a very long pause, whose extremes are
as at the extremes.
                              It is as if uncommon
ground whose extremes have no text. That
she might compose and that this might lead to

MANY TO MANY: BIG STORY

Those of us remaining on the bus no longer have recourse to the big story. Already, as it begins to traverse the bridge, the passengers fall into a *sweve* wherein their several *I*s become ball-bearings floating freely in the roof, a concatenation of little stories (neither the dialectic of the Spirit, nor even the emancipation of humanity), separated only by the Walkman's pause button. Already the *I*s are becoming *You*s, reaching further and further, till too soon it's too much. And so on and on, etc *ad infinitum* whatever happened to *dichten = condensare* for fuck's sake?

At Aldgate, Zeno leaves his seat and descends the stairwell, sumptuously apparelled. Thames glitter on a moving horizon, light brown and done in. His story over, he has succeeded in showing that the bus will never reach the opposite bank.

RAPTUROUS HAZARD

A man breathes, and breathes again. A person who is anxious to arrive but getting there slowly. Oh, so *that's* what's going on. He doesn't care what the time is nor what the idea might be. Some might have attempted diagnosis, but not he. Once might have been, got control, working through, can think about, did have the same but not madly keen. It's been a brilliant thing, yet transient and you can make something of it. It was his very much last moment.

As for her, she could need something to feel, or to deal with. That could be the problem. The marks she made in the air have faded. The thought she made in the mouth comes into being. She turns to it again. "The importance of material process over representation."

HAZARDOUS RAPTURE

He needs out, or sorted. Done no work. It was a relationship, actually charged and personal. Something actually changed. He partially goes to work, it's a book that minds him. Fired, or what? He watches them leave the room, to work or talk, allowing paper to rustle behind, or glass to rest on wood. Not enough time, that's for sure.

She's taken a deep angle to a short problem, but would like to get seriously. That could be a possibility. The catering is indifferent, but friendship flowers. She turns to it for the first time. He's jumped a barrier. Why should anyone believe her?

RUPTURED HORIZON

Walks by a stream, rebuffed and unaware of the impending. Indifferent weather might intervene. So what? Questions of scale, built on distance. Waterboatmen skip endlessly nested paragraphs. "Occlusion of the middle ground, the ground of bourgeois realism, allows the large-scale to merge with the small." A man lays his clarinet on the floor, shuffles inclement pages prior to uttering. It was very much improvised.

A woman taps on the sculpture and listens to the sound it makes. The hills slope away. Woodland enfolds a helix of rapid transformations. Mingling with others in the canteen while songsters brood on the outside. That could be the answer. A patina of rust accumulates over a period of years, allowing hermeneutic possibilities and preventing the formation of narrative.

IN LITHUANIA*

Can hear, can feel and see
and do human voices,
perform all manner of ventriloquial tricks
as though the leaves were not falling

and importunate singers
were not echoing round
with bass voice licks the vast spaces
of the ears

and rocks were not silent
nor light reflecting
on church bells tolling in the morning.

The bell is the only instrument
that does not possess the complete harmonic series.
Which is why it sounds sad.†

* Poetry Autumn in Druskininkai, October 2000.
† I am indebted to Gregory Rose for this observation.

IN LITHUANIA (2): TO THE ADDRESSEE

Thickly yellow, leaves continue to fall
upon my head. Some people link birches with banners.
Loud accordion music, *ad lib.*
A fisherman, then a mother & child
move off the riverbank to make way.

Some people, at the pink hotel.
The white riverboat. On a bench
BIELAS IS COOL. A tower
in the blue sky, extraordinary concrete.

How I wish you were here to share
this blue day that emerges. Hush.

A rustling
as of leaves that rush forever through trees.

                                        Then pause.
I shall meet you at the approaching time.

GLINTS IN A PATH

Poetic
artifice
comme il faut
the bridge
of size
(which matters not)

We have perfect
bliss to
pitch in
this
our perfect
life
as one, a pair —
too brief!

THE NOSTALGIA FOR PRESENCE FELT BY THE HUMAN SUBJECT

They've all gone
       the big stories.
Let's not mourn
       them
           we can live
and be
       without
them and within our lives

as in those outsize
           storms
in which the clouds
           and we cling
only to that —
       to us through

PLEATED GLORY

Pleated in
love & awe
        I can't
                escape I
        "know" it
but the
        mind this body's
        attached to

wanders
        to the last
day of
breathing
        which is
        the frame

PERTURBATIONS

You (a person)
at the keyboard (or away
from it). As if poised for flight
            to lee of, great hush.
The wood in that floor
with a solid sheen to it
your feet, pointed
inward

Circumambient

sour
green cymbals are stroked
with great, great gentleness (*ppp*)
to produce longing *(keening)*.

This ruins my eyes.

PERTURBATIONS (2)

...linger, petal
        we have a great
deal to do.

The sound of rain,
        or a rainstick.
A sizzle through
        the serial port.

All over the planet, a low
        drumming on wood
and some stuff
        on the E string, high...

...linger,
        petal.
Don't furl.

PERTURBATIONS (3)

Enter the poet, stage left.

I see her anew
as you pass through the door

you are so like

> His things his beautiful things
> His books his cathedral

> something that was, & no longer is.
> All fall down.

There is no
thing that may be compared. (Nothing
is comparable.)
        The trombones bark:
Vanity!
    Vanity!
        Vanity!

PERTURBATIONS (4)

"The night is blue"   and the season
a little dusty   but we begin as always
with not heeding and coming in just on the hour
in ones & twos to gather and approach
the question of intent
                              / and all those others —
For if there were no questions to cluster round
why then our skins would sink into the prevailing
gold, scribbling to oblivion.

What extraordinary advent-
ure it all is. A blue PowerBook,
an electronic skin to skim upon.

                    The moonlight, etc.
                    Sounds of birds & monkeys.
                    Sounds of the Far East.

PERTURBATIONS (5)

Perhaps sounds briefly made, or gestures
and then with the flat of the hands
so thoroughly as to come to some sort of
recognition, caressing
with backs of the hands and backs of the fingers
with the side of the fists. And was struck

by how dance-like the movement
in passion frenzy giving shape to
or suffering injury
with elbows and leaning
did not seem to refer, just hit & hit again.

And briefly standing quietly, and then again
with chopping motion, not in unison.

I would never hurt you.

PERTURBATIONS (6)

It begins here, the end of it —
You will call out
in your unknowing
at the climacteric or vertex

You were supposed to be there, and you were
for a structure'd collapsed
and everything in all directions
started uttering and had nearly blown away

You will call out, perhaps sounds
        briefly made too, with
        wooden implements who
can say, who knows
        the many kinds and ways
        the trade winds —

PERTURBATIONS (7)

Those great rich blacks come back
                              in noirish imper-
          turbable notations of the body.
The pale blue upright I appears at centre
of the screen,* there being that warmth

and difficulty. I think she grew to be broken
her eyes wide open do you remember that

lustrous silence

Immense patterns of 1s and 0s appear

there is that sound of wind
and even further away are muffled drums & a wist-
          ful woodwind theme
as if loveliness might be stepped on, or
limbs as seen close up, and slightly out
of focus. But two hundred years have passed!
          We cut to an empty†

---

* The opening credits.
† Here the film breaks.

DA CAPO, WHICH MEANS,
OUT OF MY HEAD

            On the box we find
celestial messages from splendid empires

There's been a death in the family
                        And then there was one

so madly set a thesis burned the toast
SLAM on the brakes
                        whoo —
(a paradox)

(A non-expanding universe would
            actually entail even worse paradoxes)
                        Like like like —
This is where we learn impossibility from
            This box this box this box this
                        One to one to one

ONE

Now, not why
But how — then well, not if
Why then, when not
If when, now not
If otherwise — be?
Would all then do or did & will?
Can they or it that suppose
went he though seeking still?
    west to east from
    life my change nor
    did it last, all after
    and minor, relatively third —
    it happened never, other to
    become is one

INDEX OF TITLES

Other titles in print from Reality Street Editions: